Non-profit, Tax-Exempt Corporation Workbook

This workbook is a tool to assist in the establishment and
running of a non-profit / tax exempt organization. It is not
intended to provide legal advice, but is intended to be a
place for tracking the tasks and progress in the
establishment and running of the organization.

by Amy Hereford, CSJ, JD, PhD
amyhereford@gmail.com

Table of Contents

Organizational Goals, Mission and Budget:

(The organization's goals and mission should clearly state the need you intend to address, the scope of the need, and your particular strategy for addressing that need.)

Need:

_____

_____

_____

_____

Scope of Need:

_____

_____

_____

_____

Mission & Goals:

_____

_____

_____

_____

Strategies:

_____

_____

_____

_____

Activities:

_____

_____

_____

_____

Budget

This should be a projection of our costs for the start-up and first year of operation, and for two succeeding years. An accountant can assist in projecting costs and revenues from your goals, strategies and activities above.

Revenue:	Start-up	Year II	Year III
1. Contributions			
2. Grants			
3. Membership Dues			
4. Investment Income			
5. Income from Unrelated Business			
6. Services provided by government without charge			
7. Other Revenue			
8. Subtotal			
9. Program Service Revenue			
10. Total 8-9			
11. Capital Gains / Losses			
12. Unusual Grants			
Total 12-13			
Total Revenue			
Expenses			
1. Fund-raising Expenses			
2. Gifts, Grants Paid out			
3. Benefits to Members			
4. Compensation of Officers			
5. Other Salaries & Wages			
6. Interest Expense			
7. Occupancy (Rent, Utilities)			
8. Professional Fees			
9. Other			
Total Expenses			

Excess or Deficit

Net Assets at Beginning of Year

Excess or Deficit

Net Assets at End of Year

Balance Sheet

Assets

1. Cash

2. Accounts Receivable

3. Inventories

4. Bonds / notes receivable

5. Corporate Stocks

6. Loans Receivable

7. Other Investments

8. Depreciable Assets

9. Land

10. Other Assets

11. Total Assets

Liabilities

12. Accounts Payable

13. Contributions Payable

14. Mortgages & Notes Payable

15. Other liabilities

16. Total Liabilities

Fund balances or net assets

17. Fund Balance

Recruit Board Members, Locate Resources & Develop Time-line.

Board Members

Recruit board members who bring special knowledge, skills or contacts, and are passionate about your mission. You can also list Staff and Volunteers who will help carry out the mission.

Name	Contact	Special Competence

Locate Start-up Resources

Locate those resources you will need to start your mission, money, location, supplies and equipment, etc.

Resource	Sources	How to obtain

Develop a Time-line

A time-line will help focus your plan – what steps are needed to move your organization forward? When can those steps reasonably be completed? What resources are needed to complete the steps? Reassess the time-line every month or so.

Target Date	Step	Resources

Establish Corporation

Articles of Incorporation

Adopt Articles of Incorporation and File with the State

Website: _____

_____

Incorporators with addresses: _____

_____

_____

_____

_____

_____

_____

Corporate Purpose: _____

_____

_____

_____

_____

_____

_____

_____

_____

_____

Filed by: _____ Date: _____

_____

Certificate Received: _____ Date: _____

Important Purpose Clause Language:

The Corporation is organized exclusively for charitable, religious, educational, and scientific purposes, including for such purposes, the making of distributions to organizations that qualify as exempt organizations under section 501(c)(3) of the Internal Revenue Code, or corresponding section of any future federal tax code. The Corporation may receive and administer funds for scientific, religious, educational, and charitable purposes, within the meaning of Section 501(c)(3) of the Internal Revenue Code of 1986 and to that end, the Corporation is empowered to hold any property, or any undivided interest therein, without limitation as to amount or value; to dispose of any such property and to invest, reinvest, or deal with the principal or the income in such manner as, in the judgment of the directors, will best promote the purposes of the Corporation, without limitation, except such limitations, if any, as may be contained in the instrument under which such property is received, these Articles of Incorporation, the By-Laws of the Corporation, or any applicable laws, to do any other act or thing incidental to or connected with the foregoing purposes or in advancement thereof, but not for the pecuniary profit or financial gain of its directors or officers except as permitted under the Not-for-Profit Corporation Law.

No part of the net earnings of the Corporation shall inure to the benefit of any member, trustee, officer of the Corporation, or any private individual, except that reasonable compensation may be paid for services rendered to or for the Corporation affecting one or more of its purposes, and no member, trustee, officer of the Corporation, or any private individual shall be entitled to share in the distribution of any of the corporate assets on dissolution of the Corporation. No substantial part of the activities of the Corporation shall be the carrying on of propaganda, or otherwise attempting, to influence legislation, and the Corporation shall not participate in or intervene in, including the publication or distribution of statements, any political campaign on behalf of any candidate for public office.

Upon the dissolution of the Corporation or the winding up of its affairs, the assets of the Corporation shall be distributed exclusively to one or more charitable, religious, scientific, testing for public safety, literary, or educational organizations which would then qualify under the provisions of Section 501(c)(3) of the Internal Revenue Code and its Regulations as they now exist or as they may be hereafter amended, or to the federal government, or to a state or local government, for a public purpose. Any such assets not so disposed of shall be disposed of by the Court of Common Pleas of the county in which the principal office of the Corporation is then located, exclusively for such purposes or to such organization or organizations as said Court shall determine, which are organized and operated exclusively for such purposes.

Directors and Bylaws

Name the Board of Directors and adopt Bylaws (See page 8 for board prospects)

Board of Directors

	Name	Contact	Term
1.			
2.			
3.			
4.			
5.			
6.			
7.			
8.			

Sample Bylaws are available on-line. This is a list of the major topics that should be covered, each in its own section.

- The Name of the Corporation
- The Mission of the Corporation
- The geographic area served by the Corporation
- Membership (Responsibilities, Dues, Quorum, Voting Procedure)
- Board of Directors (Duties, Officers, Meetings)
- Committees
- Rules of Order
- Fiscal Year of Operation
- Indemnification of Officers and Directors
- Hiring and staff supervision
- Procedures for amending the bylaws

Sample Bylaws

(Depending on the size and complexity of your Corporation, you may be able to simplify some parts of the bylaws. Alternatively you may need extra articles in your particular situation.)

BY-LAWS OF [NAME], A NOT-FOR-PROFIT CORPORATION

ARTICLE I ORGANIZATION

1. The name of the corporation shall be *[Name]*. The principal office shall be located at *[Location]*.

_____

_____

ARTICLE II PURPOSES

The Corporation is organized exclusively for charitable, religious, educational, and scientific purposes, including for such purposes, the making of distributions to organizations that qualify as exempt organizations under section 501(c)(3) of the Internal Revenue Code, or corresponding section of any future federal tax code. The Corporation may receive and administer funds for scientific, religious, educational, and charitable purposes, within the meaning of Section 501(c)(3) of the Internal Revenue Code of 1986 and to that end, the Corporation is empowered to hold any property, or any undivided interest therein, without limitation as to amount or value; to dispose of any such property and to invest, reinvest, or deal with the principal or the income in such manner as, in the judgment of the directors, will best promote the purposes of the Corporation, without limitation, except such limitations, if any, as may be contained in the instrument under which such property is received, these Articles of Incorporation, the By-Laws of the Corporation, or any applicable laws, to do any other act or thing incidental to or connected with the foregoing purposes or in advancement thereof, but not for the pecuniary profit or financial gain of its directors or officers except as permitted under the Not-for-Profit Corporation Law.

No part of the net earnings of the Corporation shall inure to the benefit of any member, trustee, officer of the Corporation, or any private individual, except that reasonable compensation may be paid for services rendered to or for the Corporation affecting one or more of its purposes, and no member, trustee, officer of the Corporation, or any private individual shall be entitled to share in the distribution of any of the corporate assets on dissolution of the Corporation. No substantial part of the activities of the Corporation shall be the carrying on of propaganda, or otherwise attempting, to influence legislation, and the Corporation shall not participate in or intervene in, including the publication or distribution of statements, any political campaign on behalf of any candidate for public office.

The specific purpose of the Corporation is:

_____

_____

_____

_____

_____

_____

(ARTICLE ### MEMBERSHIP)

Membership in this Corporation shall be open to all who [DESCRIBE].

_____

_____

_____

_____

MEMBERSHIP MEETINGS

The annual membership meeting of this Corporation shall be held in the month of [MONTH] each and every year. The Board of Directors shall fix the actual day.

_____

_____

The Secretary shall cause to be mailed to every member in good standing at their address as it appears in the membership roll book in this Corporation a notice telling the time and place of such annual meeting.

Regular meetings of this Corporation shall be held [LOCATION].

_____

_____

The presence of not less than _____ (____%) percent of the members shall constitute a quorum and shall be necessary to conduct the business of this Corporation; but a lesser percentage may adjourn the meeting for a period of not more than _____ weeks from the date scheduled and the secretary shall cause a notice of this scheduled meeting to be sent to all those members who were not present at the meeting originally called. A quorum as herein before set forth shall be required at any adjourned meeting.

Special meetings of this Corporation may be called by the president when s/he deems it for the best interest of the Corporation. Notices of such meeting shall be mailed to all members at their addresses as they appear in the membership roll book at least ten (10) days before the scheduled date set for such special meeting. Such notice shall state the reasons that such meeting has been called, the business to be transacted at such meeting and by whom it was called. At the request of _____ (_____%) percent of the members of the Board of Directors or _____ (_____%) percent of the members of the Corporation, the president shall cause a special meeting to be called but such request must be made in writing at least ten (10) days before the requested scheduled date.

No other business but that specified in the notice may be transacted at such special meeting without the unanimous consent of all present at such meeting.

ARTICLE V BOARD OF DIRECTORS

The Board of Directors shall serve without pay and consist of *[number of, e.g. at least 3]* directors elected by the Board of Directors.

Board members shall serve for a term of _____ years. The directors shall be elected at the annual meeting of the directors of this Corporation. An effort shall be made to have approximately equal numbers of directors terms expiring each year. *{term limits, e.g.: Directors may serve for a second but not a third consecutive term.}*

The business of this Corporation shall be managed by a Board of Directors. Board action requires a simple majority of those present.

Vacancies in the Board of Directors shall be filled by a vote of the majority of the remaining members of the Board of Directors for the balance of the term if needed to have the minimum number of directors. Otherwise the seat may be filled, or may remain vacant until the next annual meeting.

A director may be removed by a majority vote [*or a super-majority*] of the remaining directors.

The Annual Meeting shall be held at a date and time set by the Board of Directors

Regular meetings shall be held on [*frequency and time of meetings – minimum: annual, but whatever is workable, monthly / quarterly.*]

Special meetings may be held at any time when called for by the President or a majority of Board.

Notice of the meeting and its agenda shall be provided at least [*number of days, e.g. 10 days*] in advance. Directors waive the notice requirement by presence at a meeting.

The Board may meet through electronic means in any manner approved by all Directors that is free and fair.

A majority of the Board constitutes a quorum. In absence of a quorum, no formal action shall be taken except to adjourn the meeting to a subsequent date.

Any action required or permitted to be taken by the Directors or committee thereof under any provision of law, the Articles of Incorporation or these Bylaws may be taken without a meeting if each Director or committee member signs a written consent which sets forth the action taken.

ARTICLE VI OFFICERS

The officers of the board shall consist of a President, Secretary, and Treasurer nominated by the Board.

Elected officers will serve a term of one year and may be reappointed.

(a) The President shall preside at all Board meetings, appoint committee members, and perform other duties as associated with the office and generally perform the duties of President.

[*Vice president is optional: The Vice President takes the place of the President when requested, or when the President is unavailable or incapacitated.*]

(b) The Secretary shall be responsible for the minutes of the Board, keep all approved minutes in a minute book, and send out copies of minutes to all and generally perform the duties of Secretary.

(c) The Treasurer shall keep record of the organization's budget and prepare financial reports as needed and generally perform the duties of Treasurer.

ARTICLE VII POLICIES

FISCAL YEAR. The fiscal year shall be *[start date to end date, e.g. calendar year].* The Board of Directors may authorize the opening of bank accounts for the Corporation.

CONFLICT OF INTERST. Any member of the board who has a financial, personal, or official interest in, or conflict (or appearance of a conflict) with any matter pending before the Board, of such nature that it prevents or may prevent that member from acting on the matter in an impartial manner, will offer to the Board to voluntarily excuse him/herself and will vacate his seat and refrain from discussion and voting on said item.

SALARY. The Board of Directors shall hire and fix the compensation of any and all employees which they in their discretion may determine to be necessary for the conduct of the business of the Corporation.

ARTICLE VIII COMMITTEES [Optional]

All committees of this Corporation shall be appointed by the Board of Directors and their term of office shall be for a period of one year or less if sooner terminated by the action of the Board of Directors.

The permanent committees shall be: [DESCRIBE, E.G. EXECUTIVE, FUNDRAISING, FINANCE, PROGRAMS]

Committee 1:

_____

Purpose:

_____

Membership (appointment and term):

_____

_____

Chair (appointment):

_____

_____

Committee 2:

_____

Purpose:

_____

Membership (appointment and term):

_____

_____

Chair (appointment):

_____

_____

ARTICLE IX INDEMNIFICATION

The Corporation shall, to the extent legally permissible, indemnify each person who may serve or who has served at any time as an officer, director, or employee of the Corporation against all expenses and liabilities, including, without limitation, counsel fees, judgments, fines, excise taxes, penalties and settlement payments, reasonably incurred by or imposed upon such person in connection with any threatened, pending or completed action, suit or proceeding in which he or she may become involved by reason of his or her service in such capacity; provided that no indemnification shall be provided for any such person with respect to any matter as to which he or she shall have been finally adjudicated in any proceeding not to have acted in good faith in the reasonable belief that such action was in the best interests of the corporation; and further provided that any compromise or settlement payment shall be approved by a majority vote of a quorum of directors who are not at that time parties to the proceeding.

The indemnification provided hereunder shall inure to the benefit of the heirs, executors and administrators of persons entitled to indemnification hereunder. The right of indemnification under this Article shall be in addition to and not exclusive of all other rights to which any person may be entitled.

No amendment or repeal of the provisions of this Article which adversely affects the right of an indemnified person under this Article shall apply to such person with respect to those acts or omissions which occurred at any time prior to such amendment or repeal, unless such amendment or repeal was voted by or was made with the written consent of such indemnified person.

This Article constitutes a contract between the corporation and the indemnified officers, directors, and employees. No amendment or repeal of the provisions of this Article which adversely affects the right of an indemnified officer, director, or employee under this Article shall apply to such officer, director, or employee with respect to those acts or omissions which occurred at any time prior to such amendment or repeal.

ARTICLE X AMENDMENTS

The articles and these by-laws may be amended by a two-third vote of Board members present at any meeting, provided a quorum is present and provide a copy of the proposed amendment(s) are provided to each Board member at least one week prior to said meeting.

The Corporation may be dissolved by a two-thirds vote of the Board members present at any meeting, provided a quorum is present and the proposal to dissolve the Corporation is provided to each Board member at least one week prior to said meeting.

Upon the dissolution of the Corporation or the winding up of its affairs, the assets of the Corporation shall be distributed by the Board of Directors, exclusively to one or more charitable, religious, scientific, testing for public safety, literary, or educational organizations which would then qualify under the provisions of Section 501(c)(3) of the Internal Revenue Code and its Regulations as they now exist or as they may be hereafter amended, or to the federal government, or to a state or local government, for a public purpose. Any such assets not so disposed of shall be disposed of by the Court of the county in which the principal office of the Corporation is then located, exclusively for such purposes or to such organization or organizations as said Court shall determine, which are organized and operated exclusively for such purposes.

Adopted by the Directors at their meeting on _____

Signature:

Print Name:

_____

Federal Tax Filings

EIN

Obtain an EIN - Tax ID number by filing form SS-4 with the IRS

_____

_____

_____

Tax Exemption

Obtain Tax Exempt status by filing Form 1023 or 1023 EZ with the IRS (see appendix) - time-line

Target Date	Step	Resources

Sent to IRS: _____

Determination letter: _____

Conflict of Interest

Establish a Conflict of Interest Policy – sample policies may be found on the web:

http://www.irs.gov/instructions/i1023/ar03.html

http://www.npcm.com/Resources/IRSConflictofInterestPolicy/tabid/63/Default.aspx

_____

_____

_____

_____

_____

_____

_____

_____

_____

_____

_____

_____

_____

_____

_____

_____

_____

_____

_____

_____

_____

_____

_____

_____

_____

_____

_____

Establish financial management

A corporate bank account

_____

_____

_____

_____

_____

An accounting system

Adequate for:

Organizational Management
_____

_____

Tax Reporting (Form 990, 990EZ or 990N)
_____

_____

Grant Tracking
_____

_____

Substantiation letters to contributors
_____

_____

Meaningful financial oversight
_____

_____

Internal Controls
_____

_____

_____

_____

_____

_____

_____

_____

State Obligations

1. Contact the state tax board for information about obtaining a state tax number and see if additional information must be submitted for state tax exemption from income tax and sales tax, etc.

_____

_____

_____

_____

_____

2. Check with the state department of consumer affairs or business licensing to obtain any required business licenses or permits.

_____

_____

_____

_____

_____

3. Contact the state Attorney General's Office to see if charitable or solicitation registration or reporting is required.

_____

_____

_____

_____

_____

Other Steps and Obligations

Workers' Compensation

Find out about workers' compensation if you will have employees.

_____

_____

_____

_____

_____

_____

Protect your trade name

_____

_____

_____

_____

Marketing & Communication

Order any required notices (advertisements you have to place) of your intent to begin operating in the community.

_____

_____

_____

_____

Check zoning laws.

_____

_____

_____

_____

_____

Licenses & Permits

Obtain city and/or county business licenses or permits.

_____

_____

_____

_____

_____

Insurance

Get adequate insurance or a rider to a homeowner's policy.

_____

_____

_____

_____

_____

Payroll

Get tax information for employees, including guidelines for withholding taxes, information on hiring independent contractors, etc.

_____

_____

_____

_____

_____

Apply for a federal non-profit mailing permit.

_____

_____

_____

_____

_____

Order business cards and stationery.

_____

_____

_____

_____

_____

_____

_____

_____

Get an email address, phone number, mailing address.

_____

_____

_____

_____

_____

Set up your website.

_____

_____

_____

_____

_____

_____

_____

_____

_____

Annual Checklist

Develop a Corporation Checklist of legal requirements for operation including:

_____

_____

_____

Board Meetings

_____

_____

_____

Annual Meeting

_____

_____

_____

_____

Program Review

_____

_____

_____

Budget Approval

_____

_____

_____

Appoint Board Members

_____

_____

_____

Elect Officers

_____

_____

_____

_____

_____

_____

_____

_____

_____

_____

Federal Tax Filings:

_____

_____

_____

Form 990, 990EZ or 990N (http://efile.form990.org/)

_____

_____

_____

Employment Tax

_____

_____

_____

_____

State Filings

Corporation

_____

_____

_____

Tax

_____

_____

_____

Charitable Solicitation

_____

_____

_____

_____

Ongoing steps to develop the Corporation

Educate and Assess the Board

_____

_____

_____

_____

_____

Select, educate and evaluate the Director and key staff

_____

_____

_____

_____

_____

_____

_____

Develop a strategic plan

Review vision and mission

_____

_____

_____

_____

_____

_____

_____

Review programs and activities

_____

_____

_____

_____

Review financials, fund-raising and legal compliance

_____

_____

_____

_____

_____

Identify areas of growth and stagnation in the Corporation

_____

_____

_____

_____

_____

Examine areas of possibilities for growth and needed services

_____

_____

_____

_____

Board Minutes Form:

1. Roll Call.

Date/Time: Place: _____

Present: _____

_____

2. Review and acceptance of the minutes of the preceding meeting.

_____

_____

3. Reports of Committees.

_____

_____

_____

_____

_____

_____

_____

_____

4. Reports of Officers.

_____

_____

_____

_____

_____

5. Old and Unfinished Business (record any decisions precisely: motions, seconds, votes).

_____

_____

_____

_____

_____

6. New Business (record decisions precisely).

_____

7. Adjournments
8. Working Summary:

Next Meeting: Date: Time: Location:

Action items: Due: Responsible:

1.

_____

2.

_____

3.

_____

4.

_____

5.

_____

6.

_____

7.

_____

8.

_____

Form **1023-EZ**

(June 2014)

Department of the Treasury
Internal Revenue Service

Streamlined Application for Recognition of Exemption Under Section 501(c)(3) of the Internal Revenue Code

OMB No. 1545-0056

▶ **Do not enter social security numbers on this form as it may be made public.**
▶ **Information about Form 1023-EZ and its separate instructions is at *www.irs.gov/form1023*.**

Note: *If exempt status is approved, this application will be open for public inspection.*

☐ Check this box to attest that you have completed the Form 1023-EZ Eligibility Worksheet in the current instructions, are eligible to apply for exemption using Form 1023-EZ, and have read and understand the requirements to be exempt under section 501(c)(3).

Part I — Identification of Applicant

1a Full Name of Organization

b Address (number, street, and room/suite). If a P.O. box, see instructions. | **c** City | **d** State | **e** Zip Code + 4

2 Employer Identification Number | **3** Month Tax Year Ends (MM) | **4** Person to Contact if More Information is Needed

5 Contact Telephone Number | **6** Fax Number (optional) | **7** User Fee Submitted

8 List the names, titles, and mailing addresses of your officers, directors, and/or trustees. (If you have more than five, see instructions.)

| First Name: | Last Name: | Title: | |
| Street Address: | City: | State: | Zip Code + 4: |

| First Name: | Last Name: | Title: | |
| Street Address: | City: | State: | Zip Code + 4: |

| First Name: | Last Name: | Title: | |
| Street Address: | City: | State: | Zip Code + 4: |

| First Name: | Last Name: | Title: | |
| Street Address: | City: | State: | Zip Code + 4: |

| First Name: | Last Name: | Title: | |
| Street Address: | City: | State: | Zip Code + 4: |

9 a Organization's Website (if available):

b Organization's Email (optional):

Part II — Organizational Structure

1 To file this form, you must be a corporation, an unincorporated association, or a trust. **Check the box** for the type of organization.

☐ Corporation ☑ Unincorporated association ☐ Trust

2 ☐ **Check this box** to attest that you have the organizing document necessary for the organizational structure indicated above. (See the instructions for an explanation of **necessary organizing documents**.)

3 Date incorporated if a corporation, or formed if other than a corporation (MMDDYYYY): _____

4 State of incorporation or other formation: _____

5 Section 501(c)(3) requires that your organizing document must limit your purposes to one or more exempt purposes within section 501(c)(3).

☐ **Check this box** to attest that your organizing document contains this limitation.

6 Section 501(c)(3) requires that your organizing document must not expressly empower you to engage, otherwise than as an insubstantial part of your activities, in activities that in themselves are not in furtherance of one or more exempt purposes.

☐ **Check this box** to attest that your organizing document does not expressly empower you to engage, otherwise than as an insubstantial part of your activities, in activities that in themselves are not in furtherance of one or more exempt purposes.

7 Section 501(c)(3) requires that your organizing document must provide that upon dissolution, your remaining assets be used exclusively for section 501(c)(3) exempt purposes. Depending on your entity type and the state in which you are formed, this requirement may be satisfied by operation of state law.

☐ **Check this box** to attest that your organizing document contains the dissolution provision required under section 501(c)(3) or that you do not need an express dissolution provision in your organizing document because you rely on the operation of state law in the state in which you are formed for your dissolution provision.

For Paperwork Reduction Act Notice, see the instructions. | Catalog No. 66267N | Form **1023-EZ** (6-2014)

Part III   **Your Specific Activities**

1   Enter the appropriate 3-character NTEE Code that best describes your activities (See the instructions): _____

2   To qualify for exemption as a section 501(c)(3) organization, you must be organized and operated exclusively to further one or more of the following purposes. By checking the box or boxes below, you attest that you are organized and operated exclusively to further the purposes indicated. **Check all that apply.**

☐ Charitable   ☐ Religious   ☐ Educational
☐ Scientific   ☐ Literary   ☐ Testing for public safety
☐ To foster national or international amateur sports competition   ☐ Prevention of cruelty to children or animals

3   To qualify for exemption as a section 501(c)(3) organization, you must:

   • Refrain from supporting or opposing candidates in political campaigns in any way.

   • Ensure that your net earnings do not inure in whole or in part to the benefit of private shareholders or individuals (that is, board members, officers, key management employees, or other insiders).

   • Not further non-exempt purposes (such as purposes that benefit private interests) more than insubstantially.

   • Not be organized or operated for the primary purpose of conducting a trade or business that is not related to your exempt purpose(s).

   • Not devote more than an insubstantial part of your activities attempting to influence legislation or, if you made a section 501(h) election, not normally make expenditures in excess of expenditure limitations outlined in section 501(h).

   • Not provide commercial-type insurance as a substantial part of your activities.

   ☐ **Check this box** to attest that you have not conducted and will not conduct activities that violate these prohibitions and restrictions.

4   Do you or will you attempt to influence legislation? . . . .   ☐ Yes ☐ No
    (If yes, consider filing Form 5768. See the instructions for more details.)

5   Do you or will you pay compensation to any of your officers, directors, or trustees? . . . .   ☐ Yes ☐ No
    (Refer to the instructions for a definition of **compensation**.)

6   Do you or will you donate funds to or pay expenses for individual(s)? . . . .   ☐ Yes ☐ No

7   Do you or will you conduct activities or provide grants or other assistance to individual(s) or organization(s) outside the United States? . . . .   ☐ Yes ☐ No

8   Do you or will you engage in financial transactions (for example, loans, payments, rents, etc.) with any of your officers, directors, or trustees, or any entities they own or control? . . . .   ☐ Yes ☐ No

9   Do you or will you have unrelated business gross income of $1,000 or more during a tax year? . . . . . .   ☐ Yes ☐ No

10 Do you or will you operate bingo or other gaming activities? . . . .   ☐ Yes ☐ No

11 Do you or will you provide disaster relief? . . . .   ☐ Yes ☐ No

Part IV   **Foundation Classification**

Part IV is designed to classify you as an organization that is either a private foundation or a public charity. Public charity status is a more favorable tax status than private foundation status.

1   If you qualify for public charity status, check the appropriate box (**1a – 1c** below) and skip to **Part V** below.

   a ☐ **Check this box** to attest that you normally receive at least one-third of your support from public sources or you normally receive at least 10 percent of your support from public sources and you have other characteristics of a publicly supported organization. **Sections 509(a)(1) and 170(b)(1)(A)(vi).**

   b ☐ **Check this box** to attest that you normally receive more than one-third of your support from a combination of gifts, grants, contributions, membership fees, and gross receipts (from permitted sources) from activities related to your exempt functions and normally receive not more than one-third of your support from investment income and unrelated business taxable income. **Section 509(a)(2).**

   c ☐ **Check this box** to attest that you are operated for the benefit of a college or university that is owned or operated by a governmental unit. **Sections 509(a)(1) and 170(b)(1)(A)(iv).**

2   If you are not described in items **1a – 1c** above, you are a private foundation. As a private foundation, you are required by section 508(e) to have specific provisions in your organizing document, unless you rely on the operation of state law in the state in which you were formed to meet these requirements. These specific provisions require that you operate to avoid liability for private foundation excise taxes under sections 4941-4945.

   ☐ **Check this box** to attest that your organizing document contains the provisions required by section 508(e) or that your organizing document does not need to include the provisions required by section 508(e) because you rely on the operation of state law in your particular state to meet the requirements of section 508(e). (See the instructions for explanation of the section 508(e) requirements.)

                                                                    Form **1023-EZ** (6-2014)

Part V **Reinstatement After Automatic Revocation**

Complete this section only if you are applying for reinstatement of exemption after being automatically revoked for failure to file required annual returns or notices for three consecutive years, and you are applying for reinstatement under section 4 or 7 of Revenue Procedure 2014-11. (Check only one box.)

1 ☐ **Check this box** if you are seeking retroactive reinstatement under section 4 of Revenue Procedure 2014-11. By checking this box, you attest that you meet the specified requirements of section 4, that your failure to file was not intentional, and that you have put in place procedures to file required returns or notices in the future. (See the instructions for requirements.)

2 ☐ **Check this box** if you are seeking reinstatement under section 7 of Revenue Procedure 2014-11, effective the date you are filing this application.

Part VI **Signature**

☐ I declare under the penalties of perjury that I am authorized to sign this application on behalf of the above organization and that I have examined this application, and to the best of my knowledge it is true, correct, and complete.

PLEASE SIGN HERE

▶ _____
(Type name of signer)

▶ _____
(Signature of Officer, Director, Trustee, or other authorized official)

▶ _____
(Type title or authority of signer)

▶ _____
(Date)

Form **1023-EZ** (6-2014)

Information copy. Do not send to IRS.

OMB No. 1545-2085

Form **990-N**

Department of the Treasury
Internal Revenue Service

Electronic Notice (e-Postcard)
for Tax-Exempt Organizations not Required To File Form 990 or 990-EZ

2015

Open to Public
Inspection

A For the 2015 calendar year, or tax year beginning **1/1/2015**, and ending **12/31/2015**.

B Check if applicable

☐ Terminated, Out of Business

☑ Gross receipts are normally $50,000 or less

C Name of organization: **RELIGIOUS LIFE PROJECT**
d/b/a:

% Amy Hereford
6400 Minnesota Ave
Saint Louis, MO, US, 63111

D Employer
Identification Number
32-0401362

E Website:
religiouslifeproject.wordpress.com

F Name of Principal Officer: **Amy Hereford**

6400 Minnesota Ave
Saint Louis, MO, US, 63111

Privacy Act and Paperwork Reduction Act Notice. We ask for the information on this form to carry out the Internal Revenue laws of the United States. You are required to give us the information. We need it to ensure that you are complying with these laws.

The organization is not required to provide the information requested on a form that is subject to the Paperwork Reduction Act unless the form displays a valid OMB control number. Books or records relating to a form or its instructions must be retained as long as their contents may become material in the administration of any Internal Revenue law. The rules governing the confidentiality of the Form 990-N is covered in Code section 6104.

The time needed to complete and file this form and related schedules will vary depending on individual circumstances. The estimated average times is 15 minutes.

Note: This image is provided for your records only. Do NOT mail this page to the IRS. The IRS will not accept this filing via paper. You must file your Form 990-N (e-Postcard) electronically.

Form **990-EZ**

Short Form
Return of Organization Exempt From Income Tax

Under section 501(c), 527, or 4947(a)(1) of the Internal Revenue Code (except private foundations)

OMB No. 1545-1150

2015

Department of the Treasury
Internal Revenue Service

▶ Do not enter social security numbers on this form as it may be made public.

▶ Information about Form 990-EZ and its instructions is at *www.irs.gov/form990*.

Open to Public Inspection

A For the 2015 calendar year, or tax year beginning _____ , 2015, and ending _____ , 20 ____

B Check if applicable:	**C** Name of organization	**D** Employer identification number
☐ Address change		
☐ Name change	Number and street (or P.O. box, if mail is not delivered to street address) — Room/suite	**E** Telephone number
☐ Initial return		
☐ Final return/terminated	City or town, state or province, country, and ZIP or foreign postal code	**F** Group Exemption
☐ Amended return		Number ▶
☐ Application pending		

G Accounting Method: ☐ Cash ☐ Accrual Other (specify) ▶ _____

I Website: ▶ _____

J Tax-exempt status (check only one) — ☐ 501(c)(3) ☐ 501(c) ( ) ◀ (insert no.) ☐ 4947(a)(1) or ☐ 527

H Check ▶ ☐ if the organization is **not** required to attach Schedule B (Form 990, 990-EZ, or 990-PF).

K Form of organization: ☐ Corporation ☐ Trust ☐ Association ☐ Other _____

L Add lines 5b, 6c, and 7b to line 9 to determine gross receipts. If gross receipts are $200,000 or more, or if total assets (Part II, column (B) below) are $500,000 or more, file Form 990 instead of Form 990-EZ . . . . ▶ $ _____

Part I Revenue, Expenses, and Changes in Net Assets or Fund Balances (see the instructions for Part I)

Check if the organization used Schedule O to respond to any question in this Part I . . . . ☐

Revenue

1	Contributions, gifts, grants, and similar amounts received	1	
2	Program service revenue including government fees and contracts	2	
3	Membership dues and assessments	3	
4	Investment income	4	
5a	Gross amount from sale of assets other than inventory . . .	**5a**	
b	Less: cost or other basis and sales expenses	**5b**	
c	Gain or (loss) from sale of assets other than inventory (Subtract line 5b from line 5a)	5c	
6	Gaming and fundraising events		
a	Gross income from gaming (attach Schedule G if greater than $15,000)	**6a**	
b	Gross income from fundraising events (not including $ _____ of contributions from fundraising events reported on line 1) (attach Schedule G if the sum of such gross income and contributions exceeds $15,000) . .	**6b**	
c	Less: direct expenses from gaming and fundraising events . . .	**6c**	
d	Net income or (loss) from gaming and fundraising events (add lines 6a and 6b and subtract line 6c)	6d	
7a	Gross sales of inventory, less returns and allowances	**7a**	
b	Less: cost of goods sold	**7b**	
c	Gross profit or (loss) from sales of inventory (Subtract line 7b from line 7a)	7c	
8	Other revenue (describe in Schedule O)	8	
9	**Total revenue.** Add lines 1, 2, 3, 4, 5c, 6d, 7c, and 8 . . . . ▶	9	

Expenses

10	Grants and similar amounts paid (list in Schedule O)	10	
11	Benefits paid to or for members	11	
12	Salaries, other compensation, and employee benefits	12	
13	Professional fees and other payments to independent contractors	13	
14	Occupancy, rent, utilities, and maintenance	14	
15	Printing, publications, postage, and shipping	15	
16	Other expenses (describe in Schedule O)	16	
17	**Total expenses.** Add lines 10 through 16 . . . . ▶	17	

Net Assets

18	Excess or (deficit) for the year (Subtract line 17 from line 9)	18	
19	Net assets or fund balances at beginning of year (from line 27, column (A)) (must agree with end-of-year figure reported on prior year's return)	19	
20	Other changes in net assets or fund balances (explain in Schedule O)	20	
21	Net assets or fund balances at end of year. Combine lines 18 through 20 . . . . . ▶	21	

For Paperwork Reduction Act Notice, see the separate instructions.   Cat. No. 10642I   Form **990-EZ** (2015)

Part II   **Balance Sheets** (see the instructions for Part II)

Check if the organization used Schedule O to respond to any question in this Part II . . . . ☐

		(A) Beginning of year		**(B)** End of year
22	Cash, savings, and investments		**22**	
23	Land and buildings		**23**	
24	Other assets (describe in Schedule O)		**24**	
25	**Total assets**		**25**	
26	**Total liabilities** (describe in Schedule O)		**26**	
27	**Net assets or fund balances** (line 27 of column (B) **must** agree with line 21) . .		**27**	

Part III   **Statement of Program Service Accomplishments** (see the instructions for Part III)

Check if the organization used Schedule O to respond to any question in this Part III . . . ☐

What is the organization's primary exempt purpose? _____

Describe the organization's program service accomplishments for each of its three largest program services, as measured by expenses. In a clear and concise manner, describe the services provided, the number of persons benefited, and other relevant information for each program title.

Expenses
(Required for section 501(c)(3) and 501(c)(4) organizations; optional for others.)

28 _____

_____

_____

(Grants $ _____) If this amount includes foreign grants, check here . . . . ▶ ☐ | **28a**

29 _____

_____

_____

(Grants $ _____) If this amount includes foreign grants, check here . . . . ▶ ☐ | **29a**

30 _____

_____

_____

(Grants $ _____) If this amount includes foreign grants, check here . . . . ▶ ☐ | **30a**

31 Other program services (describe in Schedule O) . . . .

(Grants $ _____) If this amount includes foreign grants, check here . . . . ▶ ☐ | **31a**

32 **Total program service expenses** (add lines 28a through 31a) . . . . ▶ | **32**

Part IV   **List of Officers, Directors, Trustees, and Key Employees** (list each one even if not compensated—see the instructions for Part IV)

Check if the organization used Schedule O to respond to any question in this Part IV . . . . ☐

(a) Name and title	(b) Average hours per week devoted to position	(c) Reportable compensation (Forms W-2/1099-MISC) (if not paid, enter -0-)	(d) Health benefits, contributions to employee benefit plans, and deferred compensation	(e) Estimated amount of other compensation

Part V   **Other Information** (Note the Schedule A and personal benefit contract statement requirements in the instructions for Part V) Check if the organization used Schedule O to respond to any question in this Part V   ☐

		Yes	No
33	Did the organization engage in any significant activity not previously reported to the IRS? If "Yes," provide a detailed description of each activity in Schedule O **33**		
34	Were any significant changes made to the organizing or governing documents? If "Yes," attach a conformed copy of the amended documents if they reflect a change to the organization's name. Otherwise, explain the change on Schedule O (see instructions) **34**		
35a	Did the organization have unrelated business gross income of $1,000 or more during the year from business activities (such as those reported on lines 2, 6a, and 7a, among others)? **35a**		
b	If "Yes," to line 35a, has the organization filed a Form 990-T for the year? If "No," provide an explanation in Schedule O **35b**		
c	Was the organization a section 501(c)(4), 501(c)(5), or 501(c)(6) organization subject to section 6033(e) notice, reporting, and proxy tax requirements during the year? If "Yes," complete Schedule C, Part III **35c**		
36	Did the organization undergo a liquidation, dissolution, termination, or significant disposition of net assets during the year? If "Yes," complete applicable parts of Schedule N **36**		

37a	Enter amount of political expenditures, direct or indirect, as described in the instructions ▶	**37a**		
b	Did the organization file **Form 1120-POL** for this year?	**37b**		
38a	Did the organization borrow from, or make any loans to, any officer, director, trustee, or key employee **or** were any such loans made in a prior year and still outstanding at the end of the tax year covered by this return? .	**38a**		
b	If "Yes," complete Schedule L, Part II and enter the total amount involved	**38b**		
39	Section 501(c)(7) organizations. Enter:			
a	Initiation fees and capital contributions included on line 9	**39a**		
b	Gross receipts, included on line 9, for public use of club facilities	**39b**		
40a	Section 501(c)(3) organizations. Enter amount of tax imposed on the organization during the year under: section 4911 ▶ _____ ; section 4912 ▶ _____ ; section 4955 ▶ _____			
b	Section 501(c)(3), 501(c)(4), and 501(c)(29) organizations. Did the organization engage in any section 4958 excess benefit transaction during the year, or did it engage in an excess benefit transaction in a prior year that has not been reported on any of its prior Forms 990 or 990-EZ? If "Yes," complete Schedule L, Part I	**40b**		
c	Section 501(c)(3), 501(c)(4), and 501(c)(29) organizations. Enter amount of tax imposed on organization managers or disqualified persons during the year under sections 4912, 4955, and 4958 . . . . ▶ _____			
d	Section 501(c)(3), 501(c)(4), and 501(c)(29) organizations. Enter amount of tax on line 40c reimbursed by the organization . . . . ▶ _____			
e	All organizations. At any time during the tax year, was the organization a party to a prohibited tax shelter transaction? If "Yes," complete Form 8886-T	**40e**		

41   List the states with which a copy of this return is filed ▶ _____

42a   The organization's books are in care of ▶ _____ Telephone no. ▶ _____

       Located at ▶ _____ ZIP + 4 ▶ _____

			Yes	No
b	At any time during the calendar year, did the organization have an interest in or a signature or other authority over a financial account in a foreign country (such as a bank account, securities account, or other financial account)?	**42b**		
	If "Yes," enter the name of the foreign country: ▶ _____			
	See the instructions for exceptions and filing requirements for FinCEN Form 114, Report of Foreign Bank and Financial Accounts (FBAR).			
c	At any time during the calendar year, did the organization maintain an office outside the U.S.?	**42c**		
	If "Yes," enter the name of the foreign country: ▶ _____			

43   Section 4947(a)(1) nonexempt charitable trusts filing Form 990-EZ in lieu of **Form 1041**—Check here . . . . . . ▶ ☐ and enter the amount of tax-exempt interest received or accrued during the tax year . . . . . ▶ | **43** |

			Yes	No
44a	Did the organization maintain any donor advised funds during the year? If "Yes," Form 990 must be completed instead of Form 990-EZ	**44a**		
b	Did the organization operate one or more hospital facilities during the year? If "Yes," Form 990 must be completed instead of Form 990-EZ	**44b**		
c	Did the organization receive any payments for indoor tanning services during the year?	**44c**		
d	If "Yes" to line 44c, has the organization filed a Form 720 to report these payments? If "No," provide an explanation in Schedule O	**44d**		
45a	Did the organization have a controlled entity within the meaning of section 512(b)(13)?	**45a**		
b	Did the organization receive any payment from or engage in any transaction with a controlled entity within the meaning of section 512(b)(13)? If "Yes," Form 990 and Schedule R may need to be completed instead of Form 990-EZ (see instructions)	**45b**		

		Yes	No
46	Did the organization engage, directly or indirectly, in political campaign activities on behalf of or in opposition to candidates for public office? If "Yes," complete Schedule C, Part I **46**		

Part VI **Section 501(c)(3) organizations only**

All section 501(c)(3) organizations must answer questions 47–49b and 52, and complete the tables for lines 50 and 51.

Check if the organization used Schedule O to respond to any question in this Part VI . . . . ☐

		Yes	No
47	Did the organization engage in lobbying activities or have a section 501(h) election in effect during the tax year? If "Yes," complete Schedule C, Part II **47**		
48	Is the organization a school as described in section 170(b)(1)(A)(ii)? If "Yes," complete Schedule E **48**		
49a	Did the organization make any transfers to an exempt non-charitable related organization? **49a**		
b	If "Yes," was the related organization a section 527 organization? **49b**		

50 Complete this table for the organization's five highest compensated employees (other than officers, directors, trustees and key employees) who each received more than $100,000 of compensation from the organization. If there is none, enter "None."

(a) Name and title of each employee	**(b)** Average hours per week devoted to position	**(c)** Reportable compensation (Forms W-2/1099-MISC)	**(d)** Health benefits, contributions to employee benefit plans, and deferred compensation	**(e)** Estimated amount of other compensation

f Total number of other employees paid over $100,000 . . . . ▶ _____

51 Complete this table for the organization's five highest compensated independent contractors who each received more than $100,000 of compensation from the organization. If there is none, enter "None."

(a) Name and business address of each independent contractor	**(b)** Type of service	**(c)** Compensation

d Total number of other independent contractors each receiving over $100,000 . . ▶ _____

52 Did the organization complete Schedule A? **Note:** All section 501(c)(3) organizations must attach a completed Schedule A . . . . ▶☐ Yes ☐ No

Under penalties of perjury, I declare that I have examined this return, including accompanying schedules and statements, and to the best of my knowledge and belief, it is true, correct, and complete. Declaration of preparer (other than officer) is based on all information of which preparer has any knowledge.

Sign Here	▶ Signature of officer		Date
	▶ Type or print name and title		

Paid Preparer Use Only	Print/Type preparer's name	Preparer's signature	Date	Check ☐ if self-employed	PTIN
	Firm's name ▶			Firm's EIN ▶	
	Firm's address ▶			Phone no.	

May the IRS discuss this return with the preparer shown above? See instructions . . . . ▶ ☐ Yes ☐ No